HOW IT HAPPENS
at the Candy Company

By Jenna Anderson
Photographs by Bob and Diane Wolfe

CLARA
HOUSE
BOOKS

Minneapolis

The publisher would like to thank the Pearson Candy Company and its employees for their generous help with this book.

Clara House Books
The Oliver Press, Inc.
Charlotte Square
5707 West 36th Street
Minneapolis, MN 55416-2510

Library of Congress Cataloging-in-Publication Data
Anderson, Jenna, 1977-
    How it happens at the candy company / by Jenna Anderson ; photographs by Bob and Diane Wolfe.
        p. cm. — (How it happens)
    Summary: Describes the ingredients and processes used by one company to make different kinds of candy.
    ISBN 1-881508-91-9 (lib. bdg.)
    1. Candy—Juvenile literature. [1. Candy.] I. Wolfe, Robert L., ill. II. Wolfe, Diane, ill.
III. Title. IV. Series.

TX792 .A53 2002
664'.153—dc21

                                                            2001056198

ISBN 1-881508-91-9
Printed in the United States of America
08 07 06 05 04 03 02   8 7 6 5 4 3 2 1

Almost everyone loves candy, whether it's chocolate, mint, caramel, or any other delicious flavor. In fact, Americans eat more than 7 billion pounds of candy in a single year! But how do factories make enough candy to satisfy everyone's sweet tooth? From the basic ingredients to wrapping and packaging the finished product, this book will give you a behind-the-scenes look at how one company prepares the mouthwatering treats we love.

Peanuts

Peanuts are one of the most important ingredients this company uses in its candy. These peanuts have already been removed from their shells and roasted before they arrive at the factory. They are stored in huge bags—each one weighs 1 ton (2,000 pounds)!

A worker driving a **forklift** (a machine that lifts and carries heavy objects from place to place) moves the peanuts out of the storeroom as they are needed. The factory uses many bags of peanuts every day.

A machine gradually empties each bag of peanuts onto a **conveyor belt**, a moving platform that carries the peanuts along as it moves. As the peanuts pass by, workers check them for quality. Any peanuts that don't meet the candy factory's standard are picked out and sold to a company that makes birdseed. The rest of the peanuts are ready to be used in candy.

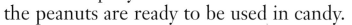

Caramel

Another important candy ingredient is **caramel**, which is made with milk, corn syrup, vegetable oil, and flavorings. These are mixed together and heated to about 240 degrees Fahrenheit. The heat makes the mixture thick and creamy.

The caramel is cooled by pouring it in a thin layer onto a machine called a **cooling drum**, shown at the top of the picture at right. This round surface slowly spins the caramel around to help it cool faster. The caramel drips off the drum onto a thermometer that tests its temperature. The cooled caramel should be about 100 degrees Fahrenheit.

The caramel travels through a pipe to the part of the factory where the candy is made.

Filling

A soft, sweet filling gives all the candies their basic shape and flavor. One of the main ingredients of this filling is sugar, which is heated until it melts into a clear liquid. It is cooled on a cooling drum, shown at top left.

The picture on the bottom left shows liquid sugar being mixed with other ingredients, including **fondant** (a creamy sugar paste), **frappe** (a fluffy mixture of sugar and corn syrup), salt, and flavorings such as mint, vanilla, or maple.

When all the ingredients have been mixed together, they form a thick, smooth, white filling.

Molds

The next step is to form the filling into pieces of candy. This is done by making a **mold**—a hollow form to hold the filling. The molds are made of **cornstarch**, a powdery edible substance that is usually used to thicken foods. A rectangular wooden tray is filled with cornstarch. The machine shown below stamps holes into the cornstarch in the shape and size that the candies will be. Then, the machine at top right squirts a small amount of filling into each hole in the mold. The picture at bottom right shows a machine piling the filled molds into tall stacks. The factory makes millions of these fillings every day.

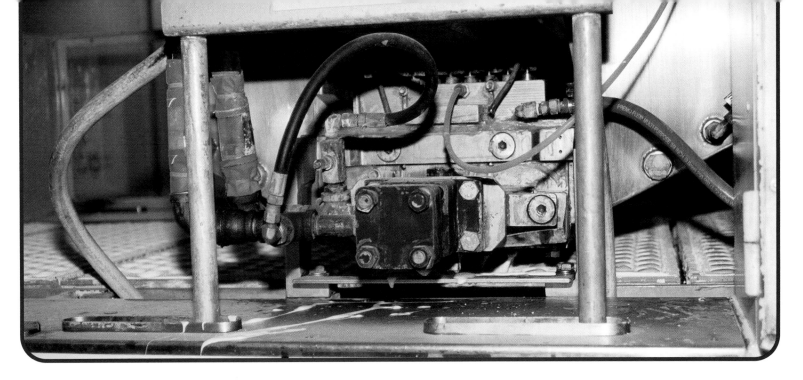

The fillings are set aside in the large room shown at left. They will **cure** (harden into the shape of the mold) for 7 to 9 hours. Then, the machine shown above shakes the fillings out of the molds. A conveyor belt carries the fillings to another part of the factory, where they will be made into finished candies.

Mints

The flat, round, mint-flavored fillings shown below are being organized into narrow rows on the conveyor belt. As the mints pass by, workers inspect them to make sure they are evenly spaced and that none of them are deformed or damaged.

The picture at top right shows the mints being covered with dark chocolate, which has been shipped to the factory in liquid form.

The chocolate-covered mints, shown at bottom right, pass under a fan that blows on them to help the chocolate cool more quickly. The fast-moving air makes wavy lines in the chocolate on the top of the candies.

Nut Goodies and Bun Bars

The large, flat, maple-flavored fillings shown below are used to make chocolate-nut clusters called Nut Goodies or Bun Bars. The fillings are carefully inspected and loaded onto a conveyor belt, which carries them into a machine that coats them with milk chocolate.

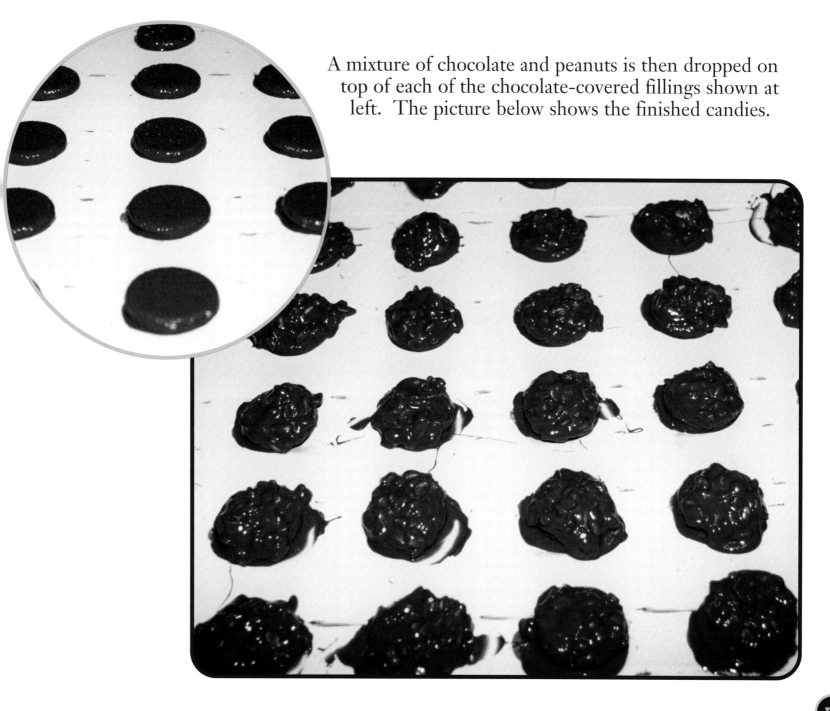

A mixture of chocolate and peanuts is then dropped on top of each of the chocolate-covered fillings shown at left. The picture below shows the finished candies.

Workers carefully shape the soft chocolate with small knives to make sure that each candy is the same size and has a regular shape.

The candies pass through a machine that cools and hardens the chocolate. When they come out, they fall onto another conveyor belt. As they fall, any extra chocolate around the edges breaks off and is collected in a tray underneath the conveyor belt.

Salted Nut Rolls

A third product the company makes is a candy bar called a Salted Nut Roll. These begin with the long, thin, vanilla-flavored fillings shown above.

These fillings are placed one by one on a conveyor belt that has been covered with a layer of peanuts and caramel, as shown below. While the conveyor belt moves along, a machine squirts a layer of caramel over the fillings and sprinkles on extra peanuts.

The conveyor belt passes through a narrow space that squeezes all the ingredients into a tube shape. When the conveyor belt widens again, the peanuts, caramel, and filling have become one long candy bar. Then the plastic blades shown below cut the candy into smaller pieces of equal size.

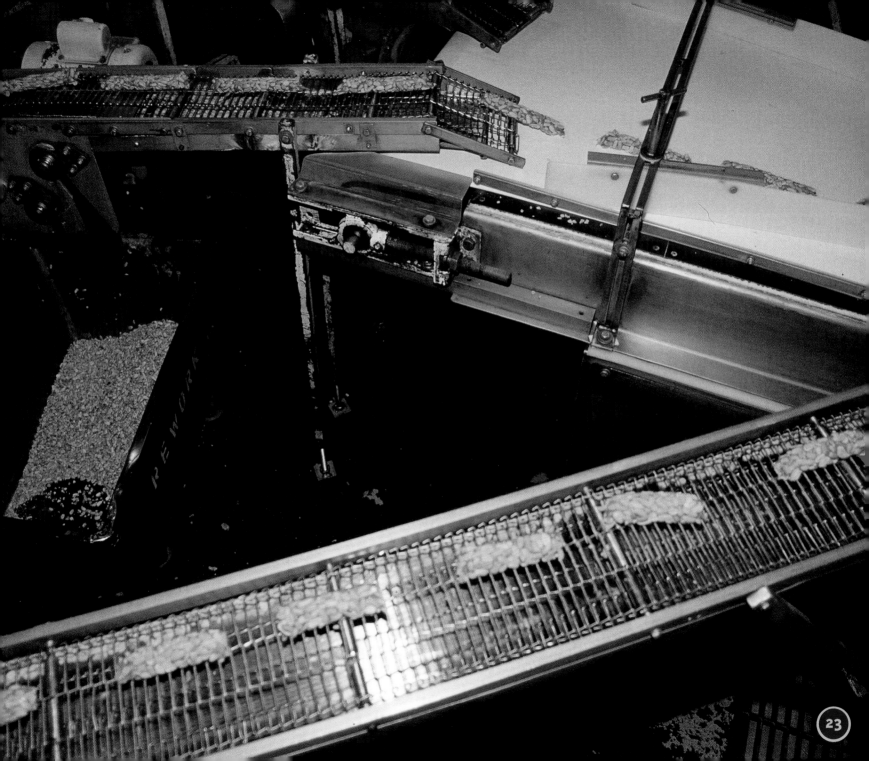

Workers carefully inspect each candy bar to make sure it is the right shape and size. Any rejected candy bars or scraps of extra candy are sold to farmers as food for pigs.

Quality Control

Every 15 minutes, sample candy bars are randomly chosen and weighed to make sure they are all exactly the same. This process is called **quality control**. Workers will also perform other tests to make sure the candy is the best that it can be. For example, they might test the percentages of peanuts, caramel, and filling in the Salted Nut Rolls to make sure that each candy bar has the same amount of each ingredient.

Wrapping

When the candy bars are ready to be wrapped, each one is placed on a small, thin piece of cardboard on a conveyor belt. The long roll of wrapping is gradually unwound and wrapped around the candy bars as they move along the conveyor belt. The machine seals the wrapper underneath the candy bars, making a long tube around them. Then the wrapper is cut between each bar and sealed at the ends. Both Salted Nut Rolls and Nut Goodies are wrapped this way.

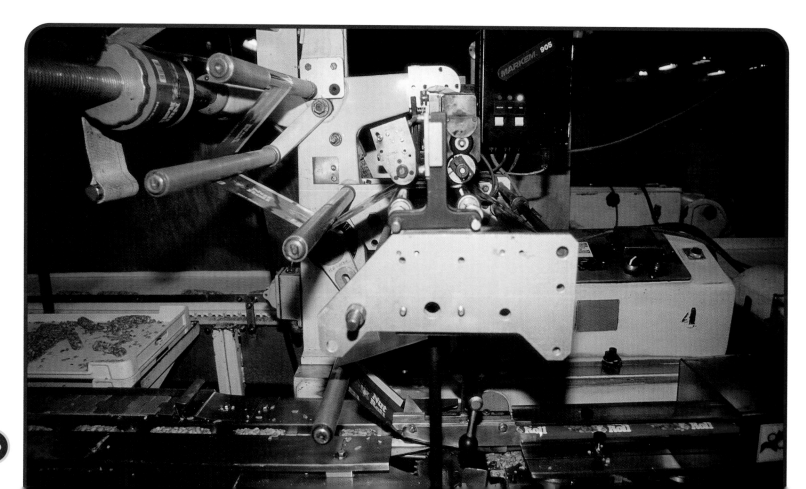

The candy bars are packed into boxes, which will protect them while they are being shipped. The workers remove any candy bars that are not wrapped securely.

The small chocolate-covered mints are wrapped by different machines, each of which can wrap thousands of candies every minute. The machines cut the foil wrapping, shown at left, into the correct size and wrap it around the mints. The wrapped mints come out of a chute at the bottom and then are pushed onto another conveyor belt.

Workers need to inspect each mint to make sure it is securely wrapped, as shown at top right.

Then, the mints go into the large machine shown at bottom right. It divides them into equal groups and dumps each group into a clear plastic jar. Other machines fill plastic bags with mints.

Packing and Shipping

In the pictures at left, the candy is packed into larger boxes and wrapped up to keep it safe and fresh. It is placed in the company's **warehouse**, or storage area, until it can be loaded into trucks, as shown below. Some trucks will carry the candy to other warehouses throughout the country, which will then distribute the candy to stores in those regions. Other trucks bring the candy directly to local stores. Soon, the candy will be bought and savored by hungry customers—like you.

Glossary

caramel: a smooth, thick mixture of milk, corn syrup, vegetable oil, and flavorings

conveyor belt: a moving platform that can carry objects from one place to another

cooling drum: a large, round surface onto which hot liquids are poured in a thin layer to help them cool

cornstarch: a powdery edible substance that is usually used to thicken foods

cure: to age or finish a product; for candy, the word describes fillings hardening into the shape of a mold

fondant: a creamy sugar paste

forklift: a machine that lifts and carries heavy objects from place to place

frappe: a fluffy mixture of sugar and corn syrup

mold: a hollow form used to shape soft substances

quality control: periodic random inspections of products to make sure they meet certain standards

warehouse: a large storage area